Gorgeously Glittery Unicorns

TOP THAT™

Top That Publishing
Tide Mill Way, Woodbridge, Suffolk, IP12 1AP, UK
www.imaginethat.com
Top That is an imprint of Imagine That Group Ltd
2 4 6 8 9 7 5 3 1
Manufactured in Guangdong, China

THE UNICORN FUN STARTS HERE!

If you love unicorns then this is the kit for you! It's packed with amazing facts and fun puzzles and includes everything you need to paint four enchanting unicorns. It's going to be magic!

Unicorniversity

In some pictures unicorns have a tail like a lion!

RAINBOW DANCER PROJECT

MEET RAINBOW DANCER

Nobody knows for sure why
unicorns are often seen near rainbows.
Some people say that rainbows are created
by unicorns. Other people say that unicorns
use rainbows to travel from place to place.
Whatever the truth is, Rainbow Dancer
has only ever been spotted near a rainbow.

Unicorniversity

A unicorn can
never be
tamed

Colour Palette

Lilac - Mix white and a little pink and blue for the main body colour.

Light lilac - Mix white and a tiny amount of pink and blue for the body highlights and the stripes on the horn.

Purple - Mix pink and a little blue for the hooves and the eye details.

Orange - Mix yellow and a little red for the stripes in the mane, tail and rainbows.

Green - Mix yellow and a little blue for the stripes in the rainbows.

Straight from the pot:

Use pink, yellow, blue, turquoise and red for the stripes in the mane, tail, horn and rainbows. Use white for the eye highlights.

Always let your paint dry before adding glitter.

SOMETHING MAGICAL

See if you can find
the mini-grid pattern
hidden somewhere in
the large grid.

UNICORN HORN

Can you find a single HORN hidden in this word grid?

```
H N R H H O O N H H N O
R O H N O O N H O H O N
O R R O H H N O R O H R
N O H H O O H N H R O H
H H O N N R H O N R N O
O R R H N O R H H O R H
R O N O R R O H O R H N
  O O H O N N O R N R
```

STARBEAM PROJECT

MEET STARBEAM

If you want to see Starbeam, you'll have to stay up very late or get up very early! No one knows where Starbeam spends the day, but at night he is busy spreading unicorn magic throughout the forests and woods.

Unicorniversity

People used to think all unicorns were white, but they can be any colour!

Colour Palette

Light yellow - Mix white and a little yellow for the body highlights.

Purple - Mix pink and a little blue for the hooves and the eye details.

Light pink - Mix white and a little pink for the stripes on the horn.

Straight from the pot:

Use yellow for the main body colour. Use pink for the mane and tail. Use turquoise for the stars, the tips of the hooves and the stripes on the horn. Use white for the eye highlights and the stripes on the horn.

Use a toothpick to add Starbeam's stars. Dot a little paint, then drag each star's five points outwards. Add glitter sparkle!

FIND A FRIEND

Can you find all of these forest animals
hiding in the grid?

```
S  H  E  D  G  O  W  L  C  B
L  K  T  A  B  B  I  H  E  R
P  C  U  B  A  D  G  E  R  P
I  C  E  N  F  O  B  D  I  B
G  O  R  O  K  E  O  G  L  A
E  R  X  C  A  E  F  E  E  D
O  A  K  R  C  R  R  H  R  G
N  C  U  E  C  X  O  O  R  F
P  C  N  V  O  M  G  G  I  I
X  O  D  A  M  S  O  O  U  X
S  O  O  E  X  O  K  U  Q  I
K  N  J  B  E  X  L  U  S  P
T  I  B  B  A  R  D  E  E  E
```

I love my
forest
friends!

SQUIRREL	MOLE	BEAR
DEER	MOUSE	FOX
RACCOON	SKUNK	FROG
BADGER	OWL	RABBIT
HEDGEHOG	BEAVER	PIGEON

THE NAME GAME

What is Princess Thea's unicorn friend called? Find the common letter on each line of names, and then use them to spell the unicorn's name.

Nutmeg	Magic	Dream	Amy	
Whisper	Silver	Chico	Chip	
Sundance	Giggles	Snowy	Socks	
Seyton	Duster	Tiger	Dakota	
Lucky	Cyrus	Cowboy	Riley	

Unicorniversity

The tusk of a narwhal whale looks like a unicorn's horn, but it is actually an extra-long tooth!

12

CLEVER CODE

Princess Thea loves horses and unicorns! Use the code to work out her favourite saying.

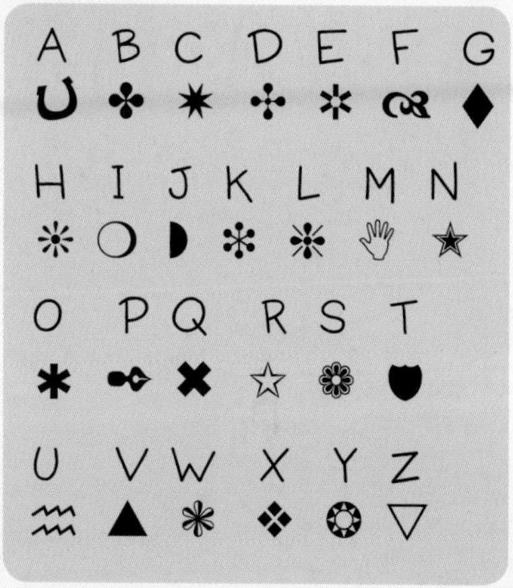

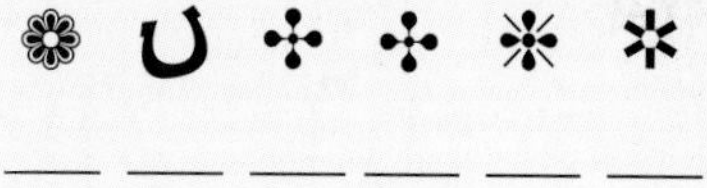

A	B	C	D	E	F	G
♘	♣	✴	♣	❊	∞	◆

H	I	J	K	L	M	N
✳	○	☽	✳	❊	✋	★

O	P	Q	R	S	T
✴	�	✖	☆	✿	🛡

U	V	W	X	Y	Z
〰	▲	✳	❖	◎	▽

OVER THE RAINBOW

Use the top picture to help you draw your own adorable unicorn.

Unicorniversity

Although unicorns are brave and strong they are very gentle and calm.

HEARTBEAT PROJECT

MEET HEARTBEAT

Beautiful Heartbeat lives on the edge of the enchanted forest. She uses her magic to protect the wild ponies and other creatures she shares the forest with. Heartbeat is probably the fastest of all the unicorns, and when she gallops, none of her four-legged friends can keep up with her!

Unicorniversity

Some people think unicorns can fly. But of course they can't ... they don't have wings!

Colour Palette

Light pink - Mix white and a little pink for the body highlights and stripes on the horn.

Purple - Mix pink and a little blue for the hooves and the eye details.

Straight from the pot:

Use pink for the main body colour. Use yellow for the mane and tail. Use turquoise for the hearts, the tips of the hooves and the stripes on the horn. Use white for the eye highlights and the stripes on the horn.

Use a toothpick to paint the tiny dots around the hearts on Heartbeat's rump.

FLYING HIGH

Although unicorns can't fly, Pegasus can! Which silhouette matches the main picture of Pegasus?

A B C D E F

MYTHICAL MOTHER

Cross out the letters that appear twice, and use the remaining letters to spell the name of Pegasus's mother.

BBMYEDYULLSPCACP

QUICK ON THE DRAW

Draw your own picture of Pegasus by copying this one.
Use the grid lines to help you.

DAISY DREAM PROJECT

MEET DAISY DREAM

Daisy Dream's favourite place is the magical clearing where the fairies live, deep in the enchanted forest. Daisy Dream has a special power: any human who sees her instantly falls asleep! Maybe it's something in the colourful flowers on Daisy Dream's coat. Don't look too closely ...

Unicorniversity

The word unicorn comes from the Latin for 'one-horn'.

Colour Palette

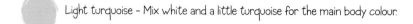

Light turquoise - Mix white and a little turquoise for the main body colour.

Light pink - Mix white and a little pink for the flower petals, the details on the body and the stripes on the horn.

Purple - Mix pink and a little blue for the hooves and the eye details.

Straight from the pot:

Use yellow for the mane and tail, then blend pink from the bottom upwards. Use white for the eye highlights, the horn stripe and the details on the body. Use turquoise for the stripes on the horn.

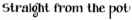

If you find stripy horns difficult, try a single colour with glitter instead!

MYSTIC SIX

Find a way from the rainbow to the little pink unicorn, stepping only on clouds with numbers from the 6 times table.

24

16   66   32

20   48   18   56

30   10   6   72

69   38   54   14

12

50   100   8

20

46   70

ANSWERS

Pages 6 and 7
SOMETHING MAGICAL

UNICORN HORN

```
H N R H H O O N H H H N O
R O H N O O N H O H O N
O R R O H H N O R O H R
N O H H O O H N H R O H
H H O N N R H O N R N O
O R P H N O R H H O R H
R O N O R R O H O R H N
  O O H O N N O R N R
```

Page 11
FIND A FRIEND

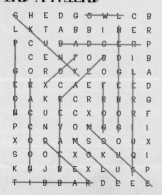

Pages 12 and 13
THE NAME GAME
The unicorn is called Misty.

CLEVER CODE
FEELING DOWN? SADDLE UP!

Page 18
FLYING HIGH
E

MYTHICAL MOTHER
Pegasus's mother is called Medusa.

Page 23
MYSTIC SIX